after you!

JANINE AMOS

CHERRYTREE
BOOKS

A CHERRYTREE BOOK

This edition first published in 2005
by Cherrytree Books, part of
The Evans Publishing Group Limited
2A Portman Mansions
Chiltern Street
London W1U 6NR

Printed in Italy

British Library Cataloguing in Publication data.

Amos, Janine
After You!. – (Good Manners)
1. Interpersonal relations – Juvenile literature
I. Title II. Spenceley, Annabel
395.1'22

ISBN 1 84234 303 3
13 digit ISBN (from January 2007) 978 1 84234 303 6

CREDITS

Editor: Louise John
Designer: Mark Holt
Photography: Gareth Boden
Production: Jenny Mulvanny

Based on the original edition of *After You!* published in 1998

With thanks to:
Charlie Jenkins, Alex Williams, Sarah and Benjamin Collins,
Charlie Simmons, Danyella Bessasa, Alex Graham,
Leon Williams, Kenneth Lycett and Bobby

And special thanks to The Oxford, Swindon & Gloucester Coop for
allowing us to take photographs in their Stanford in the Vale store.

Going to the Park

Alex and Charlie are going to the park.

Come on!

4

They are in a hurry to start their game.

The boys reach the park gate.

6

Charlie pushes through.

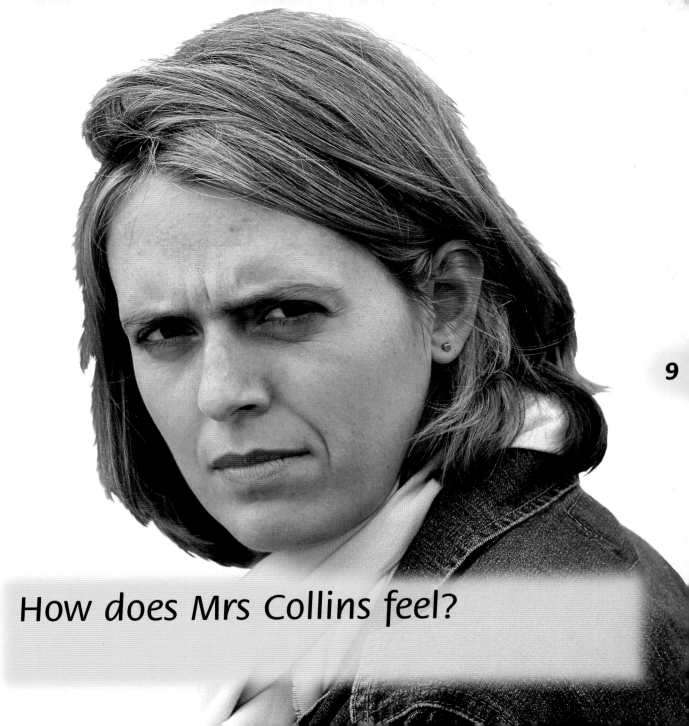

How does Mrs Collins feel?

Alex catches up with his friend.

12

Painting a Picture

Will and Jessica are painting.

They both go to wash their brushes.

The paintings are spoilt.

Will and Jessica start again.

18

Will thinks about it.

At the Shop

Sophie and Molly want to buy some sweets.

The shop is busy.

The big boys take his turn.

How does Mr Jones feel?

After you.

The girls think about Mr Jones.
They let him go first.

How does Mr Jones feel now?

It makes things easier if someone waits.

Saying After you! tells the other person you'll wait. It shows them you care.

TEACHER'S NOTES

By reading these books with young children and inviting them to answer the questions posed in the text the children can actively work towards aspects of the PSHE and Citizenship curriculum.

Develop confidence and responsibility and making the most of their abilities by
- recognising what they like and dislike, what is fair and unfair and what is right and wrong
- to share their opinions on things that matter to them and explain their views
- to recognise, name and deal with their feelings in a positive way

Develop good relationships and respecting the differences between people
- to recognise how their behaviour affects others
- to listen to other people and play and work co-operatively
- to identify and respect the differences and similarities between people

By using some simple follow up and extension activities, children can also work towards

Citizenship KS1
- to recognise choices they can make and recognise the difference between right and wrong.

EXTENSION ACTIVITY
Choice Charts
- Sit the children on a mat with a flip chart at child height.
- Read through the first of the three stories in the book with the children and ask the children the questions in the text. Invite answers and scribe their answers to 'How does Mrs Collins feel?' in a column on the right side of the paper. Add simple face drawings if appropriate.
- When asking the second question 'How does Mrs Collins feel now?' list the childrens' answers in a column to the left.
- At the end of the story ask the children to identify the action that Alex chose to take that changed how Mrs Collins felt. 'What did Alex choose to do?'
- Now, ask the children what choice Charlie made and the result of that choice.
- On another sheet of paper write Mrs Collins in the centre. Ask the children what choices Mrs Collins could have made when Charlie pushed through. Write each answer and connect it to Mrs Collins' name with a line to create a spider diagram. When all the ideas are exhausted, return to each possible choice in turn and ask 'What would have happened if Mrs Collins had done this?' Encourage the children to think through the consequences for Alex, Charlie and Mrs Collins.
- Finally, return to the last picture in the story of Alex catching up with Charlie. On a sheet of paper write Alex's name in the centre and ask the children what choices Alex has now. Choices may include 'play football' or 'tell Charlie off'. Write all the choices in a spider format around the name and ask the children to consider the consequences of each choice in turn and think about which would have been the best one for Alex to make.

These choice chart activities can be repeated on subsequent days with the other two stories in the book or with other stories from the series.